THE POETRY OF RHENIUM

The Poetry of Rhenium

Walter the Educator

Silent King Books

SILENT KING BOOKS

SKB

Copyright © 2024 by Walter the Educator

All rights reserved. No part of this book may be reproduced in any manner whatsoever without written permission except in the case of brief quotations embodied in critical articles and reviews.

First Printing, 2024

Disclaimer
This book is a literary work; poems are not about specific persons, locations, situations, and/or circumstances unless mentioned in a historical context. This book is for entertainment and informational purposes only. The author and publisher offer this information without warranties expressed or implied. No matter the grounds, neither the author nor the publisher will be accountable for any losses, injuries, or other damages caused by the reader's use of this book. The use of this book acknowledges an understanding and acceptance of this disclaimer.

dedicated to all the chemistry lovers, like myself, across the world

RHENIUM

In the depths of earth, where secrets lie,

RHENIUM

Where atoms dance and elements vie,

RHENIUM

There dwells a metal, rare and divine,

RHENIUM

A tale of Rhenium, let me entwine.

RHENIUM

With atomic number seventy-five,

RHENIUM

In periodic table's vibrant hive,

RHENIUM

Rhenium sits, regal and strong,

RHENIUM

In nature's symphony, it belongs.

RHENIUM

A lustrous metal, silvery sheen,

RHENIUM

In noble alloys, it reigns supreme,

RHENIUM

A catalyst of dreams, it's known to be,

RHENIUM

In chemical realms, a potent decree.

RHENIUM

In ancient stars, its journey did start,

RHENIUM

Forged in cosmic fires, a stellar art,

RHENIUM

From supernovae's fiery breath,

RHENIUM

Rhenium emerged, defying death.

RHENIUM

Its properties, a marvel to behold,

RHENIUM

High melting point, in tales untold,

RHENIUM

Resistance to corrosion's cruel clutch,

RHENIUM

In the alchemy of science, it's a crutch.

RHENIUM

From jet engines soaring through the skies,

RHENIUM

To catalysts in labs where reactions arise,

RHENIUM

Rhenium's touch, a magic spell,

RHENIUM

In every atom, it weaves its tale.

RHENIUM

In wires thin, conducting power's flow,

RHENIUM

In thermocouples, where temperatures glow,

RHENIUM

Rhenium whispers secrets profound,

RHENIUM

In every application, it can be found.

RHENIUM

But beyond the lab, in poetic flight,

RHENIUM

Rhenium dances in the starry night,

RHENIUM

Its essence captured in words divine,

RHENIUM

A poet's muse, a rare design.

RHENIUM

Oh Rhenium, with your atomic grace,

RHENIUM

In every stanza, you find your place,

RHENIUM

A symbol of resilience, strength untold,

RHENIUM

In the alchemy of verse, you unfold.

RHENIUM

Let poets sing of your atomic dance,

RHENIUM

In sonnets, epics, and every chance,

RHENIUM

For in your essence, there lies a tale,

RHENIUM

Of cosmic journeys and atoms' sail.

RHENIUM

So let us raise our pens on high,

RHENIUM

And to Rhenium, let us testify,

RHENIUM

In words unique, our homage pay,

RHENIUM

To the element that lights our way.

RHENIUM

ABOUT THE CREATOR

Walter the Educator is one of the pseudonyms for Walter Anderson. Formally educated in Chemistry, Business, and Education, he is an educator, an author, a diverse entrepreneur, and he is the son of a disabled war veteran. "Walter the Educator" shares his time between educating and creating. He holds interests and owns several creative projects that entertain, enlighten, enhance, and educate, hoping to inspire and motivate you.

Follow, find new works, and stay up to date
with Walter the Educator™
at WaltertheEducator.com

www.ingramcontent.com/pod-product-compliance
Lightning Source LLC
LaVergne TN
LVHW021240080526
838199LV00088B/5206